Operational

Leadership: Building and Leading High-Performing Teams

Daniel Robosky

First Edition published by 2023

Copyright © 2023 by Daniel Robosky

All rights reserved. No part of this publication may be reproduced, stored or transmitted in any form or by any means, electronic, mechanical, photocopying, recording, scanning, or otherwise without written permission from the publisher. It is illegal to copy this book, post it to a website, or distribute it by any other means without permission.

Daniel Robosky asserts the moral right to be identified as the author of this work.

First Edition

One

Chapter 1: Introduction

In a world that is rapidly changing and evolving, one thing remains constant: the necessity for effective leadership. In the business context, leadership is the driving force that propels organizations towards their goals, navigates them through periods of uncertainty, and binds individuals together to work collectively for a common purpose. However, leadership is not a monolithic concept. It is multi-faceted, varied, and dynamic. Among its many forms, one of the most pivotal yet often underappreciated is operational leadership.

Operational leadership plays an indispensable role in organizations of all shapes and sizes, across all industries and geographies. It is the bridge that connects strategic vision to tactical execution, the glue that holds day-to-day operations together, and the catalyst that drives efficiency, effectiveness, and ultimately, organizational success.

This book, "Operational Leadership: Building and Leading High-Performing Teams," sets out to demystify the concept of operational leadership and provide practical insights and guidance for aspiring and established operational leaders alike. Through the pages of this book, you will explore what operational leadership entails, why it is so important, and how it differs from – and complements – other forms of leadership, such as strategic leadership.

The book will then guide you through the process of building and leading high-performing teams, offering tangible tips, real-world case studies, and scientifically-backed theories. From understanding the anatomy of high-performing teams and cultivating a strong team culture to enhancing communication, motivation, and engagement within the team, the book will equip you with the tools and knowledge necessary to thrive as an operational leader.

Finally, you will delve into the crucial aspects of measuring and enhancing performance, learning how to design effective appraisal systems, foster a culture of innovation, and leverage the power of technology in operational leadership.

As you embark on this journey of exploring and mastering operational leadership, it is my hope that you will find the insights and lessons in this book valuable – not just in the context of your professional life, but also in your personal development as a leader. After all, leadership is not confined to the four walls of the office but permeates every aspect of our lives.

Welcome to the fascinating world of operational leadership. Let's begin this journey together.

Two

Chapter 2 : Unveiling Operational Leadership

What is Operational Leadership?

Operational leadership represents a key aspect of managing and directing organizations. This form of leadership is concerned with how leaders manage the day-to-day operations of the organization, overseeing processes, driving efficiency, and ensuring all systems are running smoothly and effectively. Operational leaders provide the structure and systemization that allow an organization to function optimally.

At its core, operational leadership is about executing the strategic plan of the organization. It is about delivering the day-to-day activities that enable the

Chapter 2 : Unveiling Operational Leadership 9

company to achieve its objectives. Operational leaders translate the organization's vision and strategy into practical, actionable plans. They are responsible for making sure that the right people are in the right roles, that they have the resources they need, and that they understand and are aligned with the company's direction.

Operational leaders typically have a deep understanding of the nuts and bolts of the business – the processes, systems, and structures that make the business function. They have a keen eye for detail and the ability to monitor a vast range of tasks to ensure the organization stays on track.

The Importance of Operational Leadership

The importance of operational leadership cannot be overstated. Operational leaders play a crucial role in the overall success of an organization. They ensure that the business runs smoothly on a day-to-day basis and that the company's objectives are met.

1. **Execution of Strategy**: Operational leaders are responsible for the execution of the organization's strategy. They translate the strategic goals into actionable plans and manage the daily operations to ensure these goals are achieved. Without effective

operational leadership, there may be a disconnect between the company's strategy and its execution, leading to inefficiency and unmet objectives.

2. **Efficiency and Productivity**: Operational leaders drive efficiency and productivity within the organization. They manage resources, streamline processes, and implement systems to ensure that operations are running as smoothly and efficiently as possible. Operational leadership ensures that no resources are wasted and that all efforts are directed towards achieving the organization's goals.

3. **Employee Performance**: Operational leaders play a critical role in managing and improving employee performance. They provide direction, set expectations, and give feedback. They also create an environment where employees can thrive and perform at their best.

4. **Problem-Solving and Crisis Management**: When problems or crises arise, operational leaders are typically at the forefront. They must identify the issue, develop a solution, and execute the response plan. Their ability to manage and resolve issues effectively can significantly impact the organization's success.

Differences between Operational Leadership and Strategic Leadership

While operational leadership and strategic leadership are both essential to an organization's success, they serve different purposes and require different skill sets.

1. **Focus**: The main difference between operational and strategic leadership lies in their focus. Operational leadership is concerned with the day-to-day running of the organization. Operational leaders oversee processes, manage resources, and ensure that the business is functioning effectively and efficiently. On the other hand, strategic leadership is focused on the long-term direction and success of the company. Strategic leaders develop the organization's vision, set its long-term goals, and devise strategies to achieve them.

2. **Time Orientation:** Operational leadership is generally more short-term and immediate in its focus, dealing with the here and now. Operational leaders are responsible for making sure that tasks are completed, objectives are met, and the organization is running smoothly each day. Strategic leadership, in contrast, is more future-oriented. Strategic leaders need to anticipate future trends, opportunities, and

challenges and make decisions that will affect the organization's long-term success.

3. Decision-Making: The nature of decision-making also differs between operational and strategic leadership. Operational leaders make decisions about how to best use resources, manage processes, and execute the company's strategy on a day-to-day basis. Their decisions are often more tactical and immediate. Strategic leaders, meanwhile, make high-level decisions about the company's direction and strategy. These decisions tend to be more complex and far-reaching, with implications for the organization's long-term success.

4. Skill Set: The skills required for operational and strategic leadership can also differ. Operational leaders need to be detail-oriented, with strong organizational and management skills. They need to understand the intricacies of the organization's operations and be able to manage resources effectively. Strategic leaders, on the other hand, need to be visionary, with strong analytical and decision-making skills. They need to understand the bigger picture and be able to anticipate and respond to changes in the business environment.

While operational and strategic leadership serve different functions and require different skill sets, both types of leadership are essential for an organization's success. Strategic leaders set the direction, and operational leaders execute the strategy. They are two sides of the same coin, both crucial for the smooth running and ultimate success of the organization.

Three

Chapter 3: The Evolution of Operational Leadership

Operational leadership is not a static or fixed concept. Over time, it has evolved in response to a myriad of factors, including shifts in the business environment, advances in technology, changes in employee expectations, and developments in management theory. To appreciate the current state and future potential of operational leadership, it's important to understand its evolution.

Historical Context

In the early days of industrialization, the focus of operational leadership was primarily on efficiency

Chapter 3: The Evolution of Operational Leadership   15

and control. Managers were primarily concerned with optimizing production and maintaining order. Operational leaders were often seen as supervisors who enforced rules and standardized procedures, with little emphasis on innovation, employee engagement, or strategic thinking. This style of leadership reflected the principles of scientific management, a theory developed by Frederick Winslow Taylor in the late 19th century, which suggested that worker productivity could be increased through optimizing and standardizing job tasks.

However, as businesses grew more complex and competitive, it became clear that this mechanistic approach was insufficient. Businesses needed leaders who could not only oversee day-to-day operations but also anticipate changes in the market, inspire and engage their employees, and align operational goals with the organization's strategic vision.

Modern Interpretations and Applications

The late 20th and early 21st centuries brought significant changes to the understanding and practice of operational leadership. Influenced by theories such as the Human Relations Movement, which emphasized the importance of social factors and employee satisfaction in the workplace, operational leadership began to incorporate elements such as employee engagement, team building, and continuous improvement.

In today's business environment, operational leaders are seen as more than just overseers of daily operations. They are expected to be strategic thinkers, effective communicators, problem solvers, and change agents. They are tasked with leading diverse teams, fostering a culture of innovation and learning, and driving operational excellence in alignment with the organization's strategic goals.

This evolution has been driven by several factors, including advances in technology, increased global competition, changing workforce demographics and expectations, and a growing recognition of the importance of employee engagement and innovation in driving business success.

Anticipating the Future of Operational Leadership

Looking forward, the role of operational leadership is likely to continue to evolve in response to changes in the business environment. Here are a few trends that are likely to shape the future of operational leadership:

Chapter 3: The Evolution of Operational Leadership 17

1. Increased Use of Technology:

Technology is reshaping every aspect of business, and operational leadership is no exception. Operational leaders will need to be adept at using technology to drive efficiency, make data-driven decisions, and lead remote teams. They will also need to be prepared to navigate the challenges that come with technological change, such as managing cyber risks and addressing issues related to privacy and data security.

2. Greater Emphasis on Sustainability and Social Responsibility:

As businesses face increasing pressure to demonstrate their commitment to sustainability and social responsibility, operational leaders will need to find ways to incorporate these principles into their operations. This could involve everything from reducing waste and conserving resources to ensuring fair labor practices and promoting diversity and inclusion.

3. Continued Focus on Employee Engagement and Wellbeing:

Research has consistently shown that engaged employees are more productive, more creative, and more likely to stay with their organization. Operational leaders will need to continue to find ways to engage and motivate their teams, while also promoting wellbeing and work-life balance.

In conclusion, operational leadership has come a long way from its roots in the early days of industrialization. Today's operational leaders are strategic, people-focused, and adaptable, capable of leading their teams through complex and rapidly changing business environments. As we look to the future, the importance of operational leadership is likely to continue to grow, with operational leaders playing a crucial role in driving business success in the face of ongoing change and uncertainty.

Four

Chapter 4: Integral Traits of Successful Operational Leader

Being an operational leader entails more than just overseeing the day-to-day functions of an organization. It requires a distinct set of traits that set successful operational leaders apart. These traits not only make them effective in managing operations, but also empower them to create an environment conducive to high performance, creativity, and continuous improvement.

1. Detail-Oriented

Successful operational leaders are masters of details. They are cognizant of every aspect of the operations they oversee. They understand that a small change in one area can cause a ripple effect that impacts the entire system. For example, a shift in a production process might affect not only output but also worker safety and product quality. Operational leaders stay on top of these details to ensure nothing is overlooked.

2. Analytical Thinking

Operational leaders often face complex problems that require careful analysis and thoughtful solutions. Consider the challenge of managing a global supply chain. Leaders must understand and interpret vast amounts of data about suppliers, transportation costs, lead times, and more to optimize logistics and reduce costs. The ability to analyze and interpret complex data is crucial.

3. Decisiveness

Operational leaders often have to make quick decisions. For instance, if a critical piece of equipment fails, a swift decision must be made to repair or replace it to minimize downtime. Decisiveness doesn't mean rushing to conclusions, but rather making informed decisions promptly, even under pressure

4. Adaptability

Business environments are fluid, and operational leaders need to adapt. A pandemic might disrupt a supply chain, or a new technology might revolutionize production processes. For instance, many operational leaders had to quickly adapt their operations during the COVID-19 pandemic, adopting remote work, enhancing digital capabilities, or modifying their supply chains.

5. Strong Communication Skills

Operational leaders must effectively communicate with various stakeholders. During a product recall, for example, leaders need to quickly inform customers, coordinate with suppliers, and brief employees about the situation. They must clearly and confidently communicate to ensure everyone understands their roles and responsibilities.

6. People-Centric Approach

Operational leaders who put people first often see high levels of engagement and productivity. Consider leaders who invest time in understanding their employees' needs, providing professional development opportunities, and creating a supportive work culture. This people-centric approach fosters an environment where employees are motivated to contribute their best.

7. Proactive Problem-Solving

Proactive problem-solving involves anticipating potential issues and addressing them before they escalate. For instance, operational leaders might implement regular equipment maintenance checks to prevent unexpected breakdowns, or they may proactively manage inventory to avoid stockouts or overstocks.

8. Strategic Alignment

Operational leaders ensure their decisions and actions align with strategic goals. If a company's strategy is to provide high-quality products, operational leaders might focus on quality control, employee training, and supplier relationships to ensure this strategy is realized in day-to-day operations.

9. Resilience

Operational leaders must navigate challenges and setbacks with grace and determination. Consider an

Chapter 4: Integral Traits of Successful Operational Leader 23

operational leader whose team misses a crucial deadline. Rather than dwelling on the setback, the leader uses it as a learning opportunity, helping the team understand what went wrong and how to prevent similar issues in the future.

10. Continuous Learning

In a rapidly changing business world, continuous learning is vital. Successful operational leaders are always learning, whether by staying abreast of industry trends, seeking feedback, or pursuing further education. For instance, with the rise of automation and AI, many operational leaders are learning about these technologies to understand how they can be leveraged to enhance operations.

These traits are not mutually exclusive but are interrelated and often overlap. A detail-oriented leader, for example, needs strong analytical skills to make sense of those details. A decisive leader, meanwhile, needs to be a strong communicator to ensure their decisions are understood and implemented effectively.

Becoming a successful operational leader is not about mastering one or two of these traits.

Five

Chapter 5: Anatomy of High-Performing Teams

High-performing teams don't just happen by accident. They are a result of thoughtful design, strong leadership, and an environment conducive to growth, collaboration, and excellence. Let's explore the key components that constitute a high-performing team.

1. Clear and Shared Purpose:

High-performing teams have a shared purpose that brings them together and guides their actions. This purpose is not just understood, but it is also embraced by every team member. A team at a software development firm, for instance, may be driven by a shared purpose of creating innovative software solutions that simplify users' lives.

2. Defined Roles and Responsibilities:

In high-performing teams, each team member has a clearly defined role. Everyone knows what is expected of them and how their work contributes to the overall objectives. For example, in a marketing team, the content creator, the social media manager, the data analyst, and the SEO specialist all have unique roles, but their collective efforts contribute to the overall marketing objectives.

3. Complementary Skills:

High-performing teams are made up of individuals with a variety of skills that complement each other. These teams leverage the unique strengths and abilities of their members to achieve their goals. A product design team, for example, might include members with skills in user experience design, graphic design, technical writing, and product testing.

4. Trust and Mutual Respect:

High-performing teams are built on a foundation of trust and mutual respect. Team members trust each other's abilities and intentions, and they respect each other's contributions. This trust and respect create an environment where team members feel safe to express their ideas, take risks, and learn from their mistakes.

5. Open and Effective Communication:

High-performing teams prioritize open and effective communication. Team members feel comfortable sharing their thoughts, asking questions, and giving and receiving feedback. They also use effective communication tools and practices to ensure everyone is kept in the loop and misunderstandings are minimized.

6. Healthy Conflict:

Conflict is inevitable in teams. However, high-performing teams know how to manage and leverage conflict constructively. They view conflict as an opportunity to challenge assumptions, explore different perspectives, and strengthen their decisions.

7. Strong Cohesion:

High-performing teams have a strong sense of cohesion. They are not just a collection of individuals, but a unified group with a shared identity and a strong sense of belonging. This cohesion is often fostered through shared experiences, mutual support, and a strong team culture.

8. Effective Leadership:

High-performing teams are often led by effective leaders who inspire, guide, and support their teams. These leaders set clear expectations, provide feedback, and create an environment conducive to performance and learning. They also model the behaviors they expect from their team, such as collaboration, accountability, and continuous learning.

9. Focus on Results:

High-performing teams are results-oriented. They set clear, measurable goals, and they track their progress towards these goals. They also celebrate their achievements and learn from their failures.

10. Continuous Learning and Improvement:

High-performing teams are always learning and improving. They regularly reflect on their performance, seek feedback, and look for ways to improve their processes, skills, and outcomes. They also encourage and support the learning and development of their individual members.

11. Innovation and Creativity:

High-performing teams are not afraid to challenge the status quo and think outside the box. They foster an environment that encourages creativity and innovation, and they leverage these to solve problems, improve their performance, and achieve their goals.

12. Adaptability and Flexibility:

High-performing teams can adapt to changes and overcome challenges. Whether it's a change in market conditions, a shift in company strategy, or a setback in a project, these teams are able to adjust their plans, learn from the situation, and keep moving forward.

The above are key ingredients that make up high-performing teams. However, it's important to note that these elements are interconnected and influence each other. For example, clear roles and responsibilities can foster trust and respect, while effective communication can enhance cohesion and conflict management. Similarly, strong leadership can promote a focus on results, continuous learning, and adaptability.

Moreover, building a high-performing team is not a one-time effort. It's an ongoing process that requires attention, effort, and commitment from all team members, as well as support from the larger organization. It involves not only putting together the right mix of people and defining their roles and goals, but also cultivating the right team dynamics, fostering a supportive team culture, and providing the resources and support needed for the team to excel.

High-performing teams can drive business success by enhancing productivity, improving quality, fostering innovation, and boosting employee satisfaction and engagement. Therefore, understanding and leveraging the elements of high-performing teams is crucial for operational leaders who aim to drive operational excellence and achieve their business objectives.

Six

Chapter 6: Strategies for Cultivating High-Performing Teams

Creating high-performing teams is not a simple task. It requires a delicate balance of various elements, including assembling the right people, establishing a clear vision, creating a supportive environment, and fostering a culture of continuous learning and improvement. Operational leaders can implement several strategies to cultivate high-performing teams.

1. Assembling the Right Team:

The first step towards cultivating a high-performing team is to assemble the right people. This involves selecting individuals with the right skills, abilities, and attitudes that align with the team's objectives and the organization's culture. Leaders should look for individuals who are not only technically proficient but also have strong interpersonal and team skills. They should also ensure that the team has a diverse mix of skills, experiences, perspectives, and backgrounds, as diversity can enhance creativity, problem-solving, and decision-making.

2. Setting a Clear Vision and Goals:

Once the team is assembled, the leader should establish a clear vision and set specific, measurable, achievable, relevant, and time-bound (SMART) goals. This vision and goals should align with the organization's strategic objectives and should be communicated clearly to all team members. The leader should also involve the team in goal-setting to increase buy-in and commitment.

3. Defining Roles and Responsibilities:

Each team member should have a clear understanding of their role and responsibilities. This clarity helps prevent confusion and conflict, and ensures that everyone knows what they need to do to contribute to the team's success. The leader should also ensure that roles and responsibilities are distributed fairly and that they align with team members' skills and interests.

4. Building Trust and Cohesion:

Trust and cohesion are critical for team performance. Leaders can build trust by being reliable, transparent, and fair, and by showing trust in their team members. They can foster cohesion by encouraging collaboration, promoting shared experiences, and facilitating team building activities.

5. Fostering Open Communication:

Leaders should foster an environment where open and honest communication is encouraged. They should create safe spaces for team members to share their thoughts, ideas, and concerns, and they should model open communication by being approachable, listening actively, and sharing information transparently.

6. Managing Conflict Constructively:

Conflict is inevitable in teams, but if managed properly, it can lead to better decisions and stronger relationships. Leaders should foster an environment where differing views are respected and constructive debate is encouraged. They should also equip their team with conflict resolution skills and intervene when necessary to prevent harmful conflict.

7. Providing Feedback and Recognition:

Feedback and recognition are key for learning, improvement, and motivation. Leaders should provide regular, constructive feedback to their team members, and they should recognize and celebrate their achievements. They should also foster a feedback culture within the team, where peer feedback is encouraged and valued.

8. Promoting Learning and Development:

High-performing teams are learning teams. Leaders should promote a learning culture where curiosity is encouraged, mistakes are viewed as learning opportunities, and continuous improvement is the norm. They should also support their team members' learning and development by providing learning resources and opportunities, and by encouraging and facilitating knowledge sharing within the team.

9. Encouraging Innovation and Creativity:

Innovation and creativity can give teams a competitive edge. Leaders should foster an environment where creative thinking is encouraged, where new ideas are welcomed and explored, and where risk-taking is tolerated. They should also provide their team with the time, resources, and tools needed to innovate.

10. Leading by Example:

Leaders play a crucial role in shaping the team's culture and behavior. By modeling the behaviors they expect from their team, leaders can influence their team towards high performance. This includes demonstrating commitment to the team's vision and goals, showing respect and empathy, acting with integrity, and exemplifying resilience and adaptability.

11. Measuring and Reflecting on Performance:

Lastly, leaders should measure their team's performance regularly, using appropriate performance metrics. They should also facilitate regular reflections on the team's performance, where the team collectively reviews their performance, identifies strengths and weaknesses, celebrates

Chapter 6: Strategies for Cultivating High-Performing Teams

successes, learns from failures, and develops plans for improvement.

By implementing these strategies, operational leaders can cultivate high-performing teams that can effectively contribute to operational excellence and business success. It's important to remember, however, that each team is unique, and what works for one team may not work for another. Therefore, leaders should adopt a flexible and responsive approach, adapting their strategies as needed to suit their team's unique needs, dynamics, and context.

Seven

Chapter 7: Leading Through Change: Adapting and Thriving in a Dynamic Environment

The business world is inherently dynamic and change is a constant element. Technological advancements, shifts in market trends, regulatory changes, and various other factors can create an environment that demands businesses to continually adapt and evolve. In such a setting, operational leaders are often at the forefront of managing and implementing change. **1. Understanding the Nature of Change:**

Chapter 7: Leading Through Change: Adapting and Thriving in a Dynamic Environment

The first step in leading through change is to understand the nature and implications of the change. This includes understanding the drivers of the change, the desired outcomes, the potential impacts, and the risks and opportunities it presents. Understanding the change allows leaders to plan and implement it effectively and to communicate it clearly to their team. **2. Developing a Change Strategy:**

Once leaders understand the change, they need to develop a strategy to implement it. This includes defining the objectives of the change, outlining the steps needed to achieve it, identifying the resources required, and establishing a timeline. The change strategy should also include plans for managing potential resistance and disruptions. **3. Communicating the Change:**

Clear and effective communication is crucial in change management. Leaders should communicate the change to their team in a way that is clear, honest, and empathetic. They should explain the reasons for the change, the benefits it will bring, and how it will be implemented. They should also provide opportunities for team members to ask questions and voice their concerns. **4. Engaging the Team:**

Change can be unsettling, and people are more likely to support change if they are involved in the process. Leaders should engage their team in the change process, involving them in planning, decision-making, and implementation where possible. This not only increases buy-in and commitment, but it also leverages the team's diverse skills, knowledge, and perspectives, which can improve the quality of the change process and outcomes. **5. Providing Support and Resources:**

Change often requires people to learn new skills, adapt to new processes, or take on new roles. Leaders should ensure their team has the support and resources they need to adapt to the change. This might include providing training, coaching, tools, or time. Leaders should also provide emotional support, recognizing that change can be stressful and challenging. **6. Managing Resistance:**

Resistance is a common response to change, and it can be a major obstacle to successful change implementation. Leaders should anticipate and manage resistance by understanding its sources, addressing concerns, and showing empathy. In some cases, resistance can provide valuable feedback that can help leaders improve the change process or outcomes. **7. Monitoring and Adjusting:**

Chapter 7: Leading Through Change: Adapting and Thriving in a Dynamic Environment

Implementing change is rarely a smooth or linear process. There are often unexpected challenges, setbacks, or discoveries that require leaders to adjust their plans. Leaders should monitor the change process and outcomes closely, using appropriate metrics and feedback. They should also be flexible and agile, ready to adjust their plans as needed. **8. Celebrating Success:**

Recognizing and celebrating success is an important part of change management. It not only provides a sense of closure, but it also acknowledges the effort and achievements of the team, which can boost morale and motivation. Even small wins should be celebrated, as they can build momentum and confidence throughout the change process. **9. Learning from the Change:**

Every change process, whether successful or not, provides valuable learning opportunities. Leaders should facilitate a reflection process where the team can review the change process, identify what worked and what didn't, and draw lessons for future changes. This promotes a learning culture and contributes to continuous improvement. **10. Building Resilience:**

Change can be challenging and stressful, but it also presents an opportunity to build resilience. Resilience – the ability to recover from setbacks, adapt to change, and keep going in the face of adversity – is a key attribute for high-per forming teams. Leaders can build their team's resilience by promoting positive attitudes, providing support, fostering learning and adaptability, and modeling resilience themselves. In conclusion, leading through change is a complex but essential part of operational leadership. By understanding the nature of change, developing a comprehensive strategy, engaging their team, providing support, managing resistance, monitoring and adjusting, celebrating success, learning from the experience, and building resilience, leaders can navigate their team through the waves of change, enabling them to adapt and thrive in the dynamic business environment.

Eight

Chapter 8: Navigating Through Uncertainty: Making Informed Decisions and Managing Risks

In an increasingly volatile, uncertain, complex, and ambiguous (VUCA) business environment, operational leaders are often called upon to navigate through uncharted waters. Uncertainty can emerge from various sources such as market volatility, technological disruptions, policy changes, or even global events like pandemics. While uncertainty poses challenges, it also presents opportunities for leaders who can navigate it effectively.

1. Understanding the Nature of Uncertainty:

The first step in navigating uncertainty is understanding its nature and sources. Uncertainty can arise due to lack of information, unpredictable changes, complexity of situations, or ambiguity in interpretation. Understanding the type of uncertainty one is dealing with can help inform appropriate strategies. For instance, lack of information may necessitate data gathering, while complexity might require systems thinking or advanced analytical tools to disentangle.

2. Gathering and Analyzing Information:

When faced with uncertainty, gathering as much relevant information as possible is crucial. Leaders can collect data from a range of sources, including market research, customer feedback, expert opinions, and team discussions. Once collected, leaders need to analyze the information using appropriate methods. This might involve statistical analysis, trend forecasting, or scenario planning, among others. It's important, however, for leaders to remain aware of potential biases or limitations in their data and analyses.

3. Making Informed Decisions:

Chapter 8: Navigating Through Uncertainty: Making Informed Decisions and Managing Risks

Leaders must often make decisions even when facing considerable uncertainty. In these cases, they should strive to make informed decisions based on the best available data, their judgement, and the team's collective wisdom. Using decision-making frameworks, considering multiple options and scenarios, evaluating trade-offs, and being mindful of potential biases can help leaders make more effective decisions.

4. Managing Risks:

Uncertainty inherently involves risks. Therefore, risk identification and management should be central to a leader's approach to uncertainty. This entails assessing potential risks in terms of their likelihood and potential impact, and then developing strategies to mitigate, transfer, accept, or avoid them. Risk management strategies need to be continually revisited and adjusted as situations evolve.

5. Building a Flexible Plan:

Given the unpredictability inherent in uncertainty, flexible planning is a necessity. Leaders should develop plans that outline key actions and objectives but also allow for adjustments and contingencies. This could involve setting provisional goals, identifying possible alternatives, and preparing for multiple potential scenarios.

6. Communicating Effectively:

Effective communication is especially crucial during uncertain times. Leaders must communicate with clarity and transparency, even when the news is difficult. This includes explaining the reasons for decisions, outlining plans, acknowledging uncertainties, and addressing concerns and questions. Open and honest communication can help reduce anxiety, build trust, and foster a sense of unity among the team.

7. Building a Resilient Team:

Resilience—the ability to bounce back in the face of adversity—is a key attribute of teams that can successfully navigate uncertainty. Leaders can foster resilience by encouraging positive outlooks, providing adequate support, and promoting adaptability. They can also model resilience themselves, showing their team how to remain steadfast and optimistic even in challenging situations.

8. Learning from Experience:

Every encounter with uncertainty provides a learning opportunity. Leaders should encourage their teams to reflect on their experiences, identifying what worked well, what didn't, and why. These insights can then be used to improve future responses to uncertainty.

9. Leveraging Technology:

Today's digital technologies offer a wide range of tools that can aid in navigating uncertainty. From data analytics tools that can unearth insights from vast amounts of data, to collaboration platforms that can facilitate remote team work, leaders should leverage relevant technologies to their advantage.

10. Cultivating a Mindset of Embracing Uncertainty:

Leaders should cultivate a mindset that views uncertainty not just as a challenge, but also as an opportunity. This involves being comfortable with ambiguity, open to new possibilities, and willing to take calculated risks. Encouraging such a mindset within the team can help turn uncertainty from a source of anxiety into a catalyst for innovation and growth.

In conclusion, navigating through uncertainty is a multifaceted process that requires understanding the nature of uncertainty, gathering and analyzing information, making informed decisions, managing risks, planning flexibly, communicating effectively, building a resilient team, learning from experience, leveraging technology, and cultivating a positive mindset. While the journey may be challenging, effective operational leadership can turn uncertainty into a pathway to opportunity, innovation, and growth.

Nine

Chapter 9: Cultivating a High-Performing Team: Developing and Sustaining Team Excellence

Creating a high-performing team is at the heart of operational leadership. High-performing teams are more than just a group of individuals working together; they are aligned and collaborative, driven by a shared purpose, and capable of producing outstanding results. In this chapter, we will explore the key strategies operational leaders can employ to develop and sustain a high-performing team.

1. Building a Shared Purpose:

A compelling, shared purpose is the cornerstone of a high-performing team. This shared purpose, or mission, should be clear, meaningful, and inspiring, uniting team members and driving their efforts. As a leader, it's crucial to articulate this shared purpose, ensure it aligns with the organization's goals, and consistently communicate it to the team.

2. Establishing Clear Roles and Responsibilities:

Clarity in roles and responsibilities is another key element of high-performing teams. Each team member should understand not only their own roles and responsibilities, but also those of their teammates. This clarity helps prevent confusion, duplication of efforts, and gaps in work, while promoting accountability and cooperation.

3. Fostering Open Communication:

Open, honest, and respectful communication is the lifeblood of a high-performing team. Leaders should cultivate a communication-friendly environment where everyone feels safe to express their thoughts, ideas, and concerns. This could involve regular team meetings, one-on-one check-ins, open-door policies, or digital communication platforms.

4. Promoting Collaboration and Teamwork:

High-performing teams are characterized by a high level of collaboration and teamwork. Leaders can promote this by encouraging cooperative behaviors, creating opportunities for team members to work together, and providing the necessary tools and resources for effective collaboration.

5. Developing Individual and Team Skills:

The skills and competencies of individual team members and the team as a whole are critical for performance. Leaders should focus on both individual and team development, providing opportunities for training, coaching, and continuous learning. They should also leverage the diverse skills, experiences, and perspectives of the team to enhance collective capability.

6. Encouraging Feedback and Continuous Improvement:

High-performing teams continuously strive for improvement. Leaders should cultivate a feedback-friendly culture where constructive feedback is regularly exchanged and used for learning and improvement. They should also facilitate regular reviews of team performance and processes, encouraging the team to identify opportunities for improvement.

7. Managing Conflicts Effectively:

Conflicts are inevitable in teams, but if managed effectively, they can lead to better decisions and stronger relationships. Leaders should foster a positive approach to conflicts, encouraging open dialogue, mutual understanding, and resolution. They should also provide their teams with the tools and guidance to manage conflicts constructively.

8. Recognizing and Rewarding Performance:

Recognition and rewards can significantly boost motivation and performance. Leaders should establish a system to recognize and reward individual and team performance. This might involve verbal or written recognition, awards, bonuses, or opportunities for growth and development.

9. Creating a Supportive and Positive Team Culture:

*Chapter 9: Cultivating a High-Performing Team:
Developing and Sustaining Team Excellence*

The culture of a team has a profound impact on its performance. Leaders should strive to create a positive and supportive team culture characterized by trust, respect, inclusivity, and positivity. This involves modeling these values, setting expectations, and addressing behaviors that undermine the team culture.

10. Sustaining High Performance:

Achieving high performance is one thing, but sustaining it is another. Leaders should continuously monitor and nurture their team's performance, adjusting their strategies as needed. They should also maintain a long-term perspective, balancing the need for immediate results with the sustainability of performance.

By implementing these strategies, operational leaders can cultivate a high-performing team that is aligned, collaborative, capable, and resilient. Such a team can effectively contribute to operational excellence and the overall success of the organization.

Ten

Chapter 10: Achieving Operational Excellence: Streamlining Processes and Enhancing Productivity

Operational excellence is a philosophy that embraces problem-solving and leadership as a way to continuously improve. At its heart lies a deep-seated belief in respect for people and a never-ending search for a better way of doing things. Operational leaders who successfully implement this

Chapter 10: Achieving Operational Excellence: Streamlining Processes and Enhancing Productivity

philosophy stand to gain not only improved productivity and efficiency but also a significant competitive advantage. This chapter delves into how leaders can cultivate an environment that champions operational excellence.

1. Emphasizing Customer Value:

Central to operational excellence is a comprehensive understanding of the customer. Leaders must prioritize gaining deep insights into who their customers are, their unique needs, preferences, and values. This customer-centric approach enables the organization to develop processes that truly deliver value to the customer, driving customer loyalty and fostering business growth. Surveys, interviews, focus groups, and customer data analytics are among the tools leaders can use to understand customer value.

2. Streamlining Processes:

Operational excellence necessitates optimizing operations for efficiency and productivity. This means identifying waste or non-value adding activities in the process and eliminating them. Lean management, Six Sigma, and Business Process Reengineering are proven methodologies that leaders can use to scrutinize and improve their processes, enhancing speed, reducing costs, and improving overall efficiency.

3. Standardizing Operations:

Consistency is the hallmark of operational excellence. By standardizing operations, leaders can reduce variability, minimize errors, and guarantee consistent quality. This involves establishing clear operational procedures, guidelines, and standards and ensuring adherence to these protocols across the board.

4. Encouraging Continuous Improvement:

The pursuit of operational excellence is a journey, not a destination. It requires an organizational culture that embraces continuous improvement. Leaders must encourage each team member to consistently identify and implement improvements in their work. This fosters innovation and keeps the organization agile and ready to adapt to changing circumstances.

5. Leveraging Technology:

*Chapter 10: Achieving Operational Excellence:
Streamlining Processes and Enhancing Productivity* 55

Modern technology offers a myriad of opportunities to enhance operational efficiency. From automation that streamlines repetitive tasks, to sophisticated data analytics that provide detailed operational insights, technology is a powerful tool for operational excellence. Leaders should stay abreast of relevant technological advancements and judiciously incorporate them into their processes.

6. Enhancing Productivity:

Operational excellence seeks to optimize productivity by producing more outputs with the same or fewer inputs. Leaders can boost productivity by optimizing resource allocation, refining work methods, investing in skill development, and nurturing employee motivation and engagement. It's also essential to regularly review productivity metrics and make necessary adjustments to maintain high levels of output.

7. Fostering Employee Engagement:

A fully engaged workforce is more likely to be productive and customer-focused. Furthermore, engaged employees are more likely to contribute to the continuous improvement efforts that underpin operational excellence. Leaders can cultivate engagement by creating a positive work environment, involving employees in decision-making processes, recognizing and rewarding their contributions, and providing opportunities for professional growth and development.

8. Implementing Quality Management:

Operational excellence necessitates a focus on quality. Quality management involves planning, organizing, directing, and controlling resources to ensure customer satisfaction and facilitate continuous improvement. Techniques like Total Quality Management (TQM) and quality management systems like ISO 9001 can be instrumental in maintaining and improving product or service quality.

9. Managing Performance:

Tracking and managing performance is critical for operational excellence. Leaders should define clear performance objectives, consistently measure performance against these benchmarks, provide regular feedback, and initiate corrective actions when necessary. Performance management aids in identifying high performers and areas that require improvement, leading to informed decision-making and strategic planning.

10. Sustaining Operational Excellence:

Operational excellence is not a one-off achievement but an ongoing commitment. It requires relentless focus, cultural transformation, continuous employee involvement and learning, and constant reviews and adjustments. Leaders need to ensure that the pursuit of

Eleven

Chapter 11: Overcoming Challenges in Operational Leadership: Anticipating and Addressing Obstacles

Operational leadership, while an exceptionally rewarding role, is inevitably fraught with challenges. The ability to successfully navigate these obstacles determines the effectiveness of an operational leader and the consequent success of their team and organization. In this chapter, we

Chapter 11: Overcoming Challenges in Operational Leadership: Anticipating and Addressing Obstacles

delve into common challenges that operational leaders face and the strategies that can be employed to overcome these hurdles.

1. Managing Change:

Change is a constant in the business landscape. Market conditions, competition, customer preferences, technology - all these variables are in a state of flux, necessitating operational leaders to adapt their strategies and processes continually. However, change is often met with resistance, and managing it effectively requires a structured approach. Leaders must communicate the reasons for the change, the benefits it brings, and the plan for its implementation. Involving employees in the change process and providing necessary support, such as training or resources, can also aid in smooth transition. Monitoring progress and making necessary adjustments ensures that the change process stays on track.

2. Navigating Complexity:

The operational aspect of any organization is typically a complex web of processes, tasks, and functions. Add to this the unpredictability of external factors, and decision-making becomes a daunting task. Navigating this complexity effectively requires a systematic approach. Leveraging data and analytics can provide valuable insights that inform decision-making. Encouraging diversity in the team can bring in a variety of perspectives that contribute to a well-rounded decision. Maintaining flexibility allows for quick course corrections when required.

3. Overcoming Resistance:

Any change or initiative, no matter how beneficial, is likely to encounter resistance. This resistance can be a significant hurdle in implementing operational initiatives. Understanding the root causes of resistance is the first step in overcoming it. Leaders can then engage with those resisting the change, addressing their concerns and communicating the benefits of the initiative. Demonstrating top management's commitment to the change can also help alleviate fears and win support.

4. Ensuring Alignment:

Alignment of operational activities with strategic goals is often a challenge. Misalignment can lead to wasted efforts and subpar results. Regular communication with the team ensures that everyone understands the strategic goals and how their work contributes to these goals. Setting clear expectations and establishing a direct link between operational objectives and strategic goals can further enhance alignment.

5. Building and Sustaining High-Performing Teams:

A high-performing team is the engine of operational success. Creating such a team involves articulating a shared purpose that inspires and unites the team, clarifying roles and responsibilities to prevent confusion and duplication of efforts, fostering open communication to ensure everyone has the information they need, and promoting collaboration to leverage the collective abilities of the team. Sustaining high performance requires ongoing effort, including providing opportunities for growth and learning, recognizing and rewarding performance, and continuously realigning the team with changing objectives.

6. Managing Resources:

Operational leaders have to juggle various resources, including time, budget, personnel, and materials. Effective resource management starts with careful planning and allocation of resources based on priorities. Regular monitoring helps identify any wastage or inefficiencies. Based on these insights, leaders can adjust resource allocation to optimize utilization.

7. Balancing Short-Term and Long-Term Goals:

Leaders often face the pressure of delivering immediate results while also ensuring long-term sustainability. This requires setting clear priorities and making strategic trade-offs. A long-term perspective helps maintain focus on sustainable success, even while striving for short-term goals.

8. Ensuring Quality and Compliance:

Ensuring consistent quality while also complying with an array of regulatory requirements can be a daunting task. Implementing a robust quality management system can provide a structured approach to maintaining quality. Regular training ensures that everyone understands the quality standards and compliance requirements. Fostering a culture that values quality and compliance can drive adherence to these standards.

9. Cultivating Continuous Improvement:

Chapter 11: Overcoming Challenges in Operational Leadership: Anticipating and Addressing Obstacles   63

Continuous improvement is a cornerstone of operational excellence. However, creating a culture that values and practices continuous improvement is a challenge. Leaders can model a learning mindset, demonstrating their own commitment to continuous learning and improvement. Encouraging open feedback allows for identification of areas for improvement. Recognizing and rewarding improvements reinforces the importance of continuous improvement. Providing opportunities for learning and growth supports continuous improvement efforts.

10. Leading in the Digital Age:

The rapid pace of technological advancements offers enormous opportunities to improve operations. However, it also brings challenges, including the risk of technology obsolescence, cybersecurity threats, and the need for new skills. Leaders can leverage technology for operational improvement, but they also need to manage the associated risks. Ensuring the digital readiness of the team, through training and support, can help harness the potential of technology.

In conclusion, challenges are part and parcel of the operational leadership role. Anticipating these challenges and adopting proactive strategies can help operational leaders navigate these obstacles effectively. By doing so, they can guide their teams towards operational excellence, driving organizational growth and success in the process. Despite the hurdles, the journey of operational leadership is one of continuous learning, improvement, and fulfillment.

Twelve

Chapter 12: Evaluating Operational Leadership: Metrics and KPIs for Effective Leadership

The efficacy of operational leadership is contingent upon the ability to evaluate and measure performance. Throughout this book, we've dissected the intricate components of operational leadership, delved into the multifarious challenges it presents, and explored strategies to surmount these challenges. However, without a comprehensive evaluation of how effectively these strategies are implemented and how successfully objectives are met, an operational leader's efforts may be futile. In this penultimate chapter, we'll unravel various metrics and Key Performance Indicators (KPIs) that can serve as robust tools for operational leaders to assess their leadership effectiveness, measure their team's progress, and guide their strategic efforts towards perpetual improvement.

1. Efficiency Metrics:

Efficiency is the backbone of operational leadership. To optimize operational efficiency, leaders need to measure performance indicators like process cycle time, which helps ascertain the speed of operations; capacity utilization, which shows how well resources are used; and cost per unit, which sheds light on the cost-effectiveness of operations. By tracking these metrics, leaders can gain insights into the efficiency of their operations and formulate strategies to enhance it.

2. Quality Indicators:

The quality of products or services is a litmus test for operational excellence. Defect rates, return rates, and customer complaints are KPIs that can help measure the quality delivered. A lower defect rate signifies superior quality, while a high rate could indicate potential problems in the production process. Return rates and customer complaints directly reflect customer satisfaction with the product or service quality. Leaders can also adopt comprehensive quality management systems, such as ISO 9001, to maintain high-quality standards across all operations.

3. Productivity Measures:

Productivity measures, like output per labor hour, can help ascertain how effectively resources are being utilized. These indicators provide valuable insights into team efficiency and can help identify potential bottlenecks or areas requiring improvement. By tracking productivity metrics, leaders can ensure optimal resource utilization and maximize output.

4. Customer-Centric Metrics:

As we've established, the end goal of any operation is to satisfy customer needs. Therefore, measuring customer satisfaction is a crucial part of operational leadership. Metrics like Customer Satisfaction Scores (CSAT), Net Promoter Scores (NPS), and Customer Effort Scores (CES) provide a direct measure of how well operations align with customer expectations.

5. Employee-Related Metrics:

People are the most valuable resource in an organization, and their engagement and satisfaction are critical to operational success. By using engagement surveys, leaders can gauge employee morale and identify areas of dissatisfaction. Turnover rates can provide insights into job satisfaction and retention, while absenteeism rates can help identify issues affecting employee engagement.

6. Compliance Indicators:

Compliance with regulatory requirements and standards is a fundamental responsibility of operational leaders. By monitoring compliance rates and audit results, leaders can assess adherence to these regulations. A high number of non-compliance issues could signify the need for improved training or a revision of operational procedures.

7. Continuous Improvement Indicators:

Chapter 12: Evaluating Operational Leadership: Metrics and KPIs for Effective Leadership

Operational leadership involves a commitment to constant improvement. By tracking the number of improvement initiatives, the time it takes to implement improvements, and the impact of these improvements on operational metrics, leaders can measure the degree of continuous improvement.

8. Financial Metrics:

Lastly, operational leadership significantly influences an organization's financial performance. Metrics like cost efficiency, return on investment (ROI), and profit margins can provide insights into the financial effectiveness of operations.

In wrapping up, effective operational leadership mandates a firm emphasis on performance measurement and evaluation. Harnessing the power of metrics and KPIs allows leaders to objectively assess their operational performance, pinpoint areas needing improvement, and navigate their efforts towards augmenting operational excellence. As management guru Peter Drucker aptly stated, "What gets measured gets managed." Therefore, the judicious selection and consistent tracking of the right metrics are crucial in guiding operational leadership towards the achievement of organizational objectives. As we progress towards the final chapter, we'll revisit the fundamental principles of operational leadership, encapsulate the insights accumulated throughout this book, and provide a roadmap for operational leaders to steer their teams towards high performance and success.

Thirteen

Chapter 13: Implementing and Sustaining Operational Leadership: A Practical Guide for Success

As we approach the end of our exploration into operational leadership, we find ourselves equipped with a deep understanding of its critical aspects and the key to successfully navigating its many challenges. Now, let's tie everything together and provide a pragmatic guide on how to implement and sustain operational leadership effectively in your professional life.

1. Understand and Embrace the Role:

The first step in your journey as an operational leader is understanding the intricacies of the role and fully embracing it. Remember that operational leadership is not about merely overseeing day-to-day activities. It is about driving operational excellence, leading teams to high performance, and aligning operations with strategic goals. You have to be ready to be the driver of change, a relentless problem-solver, and an advocate for continuous improvement.

2. Build a High-Performing Team:

The bedrock of successful operational leadership is a high-performing team. To build such a team, you must start with selecting the right people. Look for individuals who have the necessary skills and a positive attitude. Once you have the right people, focus on creating an environment that fosters collaboration, encourages open communication, and rewards performance. Remember, the team's success is your success.

3. Develop Operational Plans:

Chapter 13: Implementing and Sustaining Operational Leadership: A Practical Guide for Success 73

Operational planning is a core responsibility of operational leaders. This involves translating strategic goals into operational objectives, defining key performance indicators (KPIs), and outlining action plans. It's essential to ensure that the operational plan aligns with the organization's strategy and takes into account the resources available and the constraints in place.

4. Foster Effective Communication:

Communication is a critical leadership skill. It is particularly important in operational leadership because it ensures everyone understands their roles and responsibilities, keeps the team informed about the plan and progress, and fosters a culture of feedback and continuous improvement. Foster an environment where communication is open, clear, and regular.

5. Implement Change and Improvement Initiatives:

Operational leaders are agents of change. They strive for continuous improvement and are not afraid to challenge the status quo. Whether it is implementing a new technology, adopting a new process, or driving a change in culture, operational leaders take the initiative. It's essential to manage these changes effectively, involving the team in the change process, communicating the benefits, and providing the necessary support.

6. Monitor and Control Operations:

Operational leaders are responsible for ensuring that operations run smoothly and efficiently. This involves monitoring operations using appropriate metrics and KPIs, identifying deviations, and taking corrective action. This step also includes managing resources effectively and ensuring quality and compliance.

7. Evaluate Performance and Foster Continuous Improvement:

Finally, operational leaders are committed to continuous improvement. They regularly evaluate performance, using metrics and KPIs, to identify areas for improvement. They encourage feedback, learn from failures, and celebrate successes. They foster a learning culture where everyone is committed to improving and growing.

In conclusion, operational leadership is a challenging yet rewarding role. It involves driving operational excellence, leading teams to high performance, and aligning operations with strategic objectives. It requires a range of skills, from planning and organizing to communication and decision-making. While the journey of operational leadership is fraught with challenges, it is also filled with opportunities for learning, growth, and fulfillment. By embracing the principles of operational leadership, you can guide your team towards success, contributing to the overall growth and success of the organization.

As we close this book, remember that the journey of operational leadership does not end here. It is a continuous process of learning, improving, and growing. The principles and strategies discussed in this book provide a foundation, but you must continue to develop your skills, adapt to changing circumstances, and strive for excellence. Operational leadership is not a destination but a journey, a journey that offers numerous opportunities to make a difference, to lead, to grow, and to succeed. Embrace the journey, and lead your team to new heights of performance and success.

www.ingramcontent.com/pod-product-compliance
Lightning Source LLC
Chambersburg PA
CBHW070123230526
45472CB00004B/1399